DIY · DO IT YOURSELF ·

Amazing Makerspace

Electricity

KRISTINA A. HOLZWEISS

Children's Press®
An Imprint of Scholastic Inc.

Content Consultant
Shaunna Smith, EdD
Assistant Professor of Educational Technology
Department of Curriculum
Texas State University, San Marcos, Texas

Library of Congress Cataloging-in-Publication Data
Names: Holzweiss, Kristina, author.
Title: Amazing makerspace DIY with electricity / by Kristina Holzweiss.
Other titles: True book.
Description: New York, NY : Children's Press, an imprint of Scholastic Inc.,
   2018. | Series: A true book
Identifiers: LCCN 2017011218 | ISBN 9780531238455 (library binding) | ISBN
   9780531240960 (pbk.)
Subjects: LCSH: Electricity—Experiments—Juvenile literature.
Classification: LCC QC527.2 .H655 2018 | DDC 537.078—dc23
LC record available at https://lccn.loc.gov/2017011218

Front cover: Light-Up Birthday Card project

Back cover: Student with Homemade Flashlight project

Find the Truth!

Everything you are about to read is true *except* for one of the sentences on this page.

Which one is **TRUE**?

T or F A circuit must form a complete, closed loop.

T or F Conductors are materials that block electricity from moving.

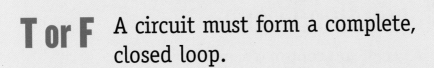

Find the answers in this book.

Contents

THE **BIG** TRUTH!

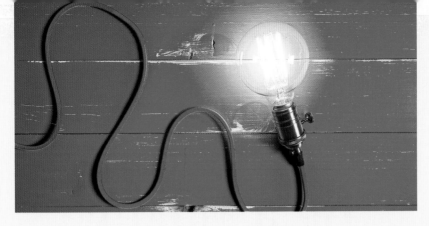

Lightbulb

Warning!
Some of these projects use pointy,
sticky, hot, or otherwise risky objects.
Keep a trusted adult around to
help you out and keep you safe.

You Can Be a Maker!

Makers are always thinking about problems and searching for ways to solve them. They create machines and test them out. Then they think about what they have learned and improve their work until it is perfect.

You can be a maker, too! This book will help you make creations that use electricity. Follow the directions to make them in your **makerspace**. Then experiment with your creations to make them even better!

Steady
Hand
Game

Homemade
Flashlight

Light-Up
Birthday
Card

CHAPTER 1

Light-Up Birthday Card

Do you like making and giving cards to celebrate birthdays and other holidays? Makers are always on the lookout for a new and different way to create. You can apply this same creativity to homemade cards. With paper **circuits,** you can combine paper crafts with electronics to create cards that literally light up. This is a great way to learn the basics of working with electricity. And you'll only need a few supplies!

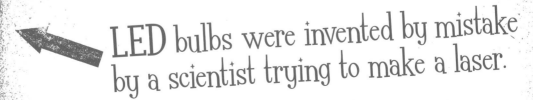

LED bulbs were invented by mistake by a scientist trying to make a laser.

What Is a Circuit?

Electricity travels along pathways called circuits. A circuit begins with a power source such as a battery. The electricity leaves the power source and travels along the path. Along the way, it might pass through **components** such as lights. This is what makes the components move, light up, or do whatever they're designed to do. Eventually, the electricity travels all the way back in a complete loop to the power source.

A lightbulb is one example of an electrical component.

TYPES OF BATTERIES

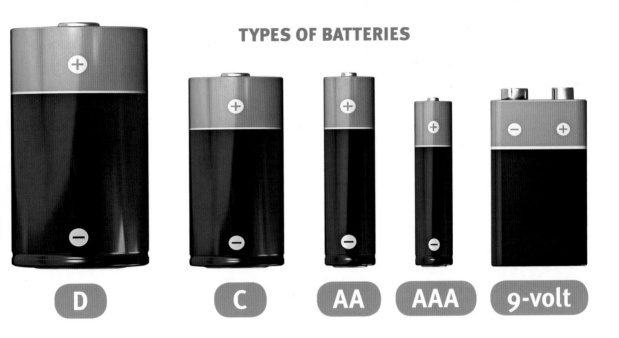

D C AA AAA 9-volt

Positive and Negative

Batteries, LED lights, and many other electronic components have two sides. They are labeled positive (+) and negative (–). Always keep this in mind as you build circuits. Anytime a project isn't working right, check to make sure you have the positive and negative sides of your components in the correct positions.

Build a Light-Up ⭐ Birthday Card

LED lights come in many colors.

What You Need

- ⬜ White unlined paper, 8 ½ inches by 11 inches or larger
- ⬜ Pencil
- ⬜ Markers, crayons, and other art supplies
- ⬜ LED light with wires
- ⬜ Clear tape
- ⬜ 3-volt coin battery
- ⬜ Adhesive copper tape
- ⬜ Small binder clip

Project Instructions

1. Lay the paper on a flat surface. Fold it in half to make the birthday card.

2. Use your pencil to draw a birthday cake with one candle on the front of the card.

3. Decorate the front of the card using markers, crayons, and other art supplies.

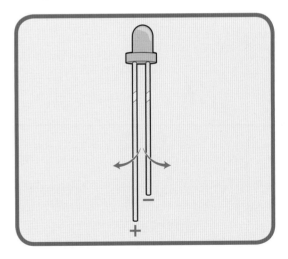

4. The LED light has two wire legs. The longer wire is positive. The shorter wire is negative. Spread them apart so they form one straight line.

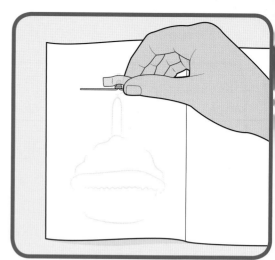

5. Open the card. Position the LED on the left side of the card's interior, just behind the candle's flame on the front.

6. Attach the LED to the paper with clear tape. Leave the light's legs uncovered.

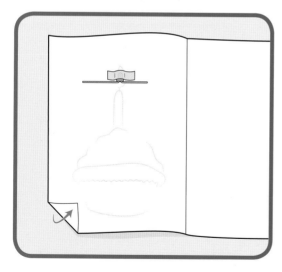

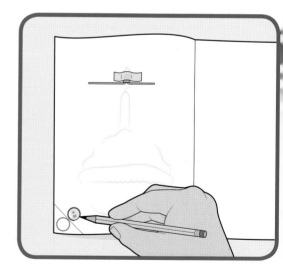

7. Fold over the bottom left corner of the paper as shown. Open it back up.

8. Trace around the battery on both sides of the crease.

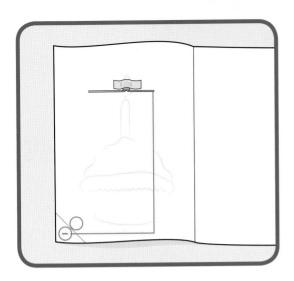

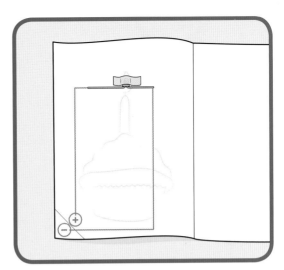

9. Draw a path in the shape of an L from the negative leg of the LED into the circle that sits farther into the corner. Mark this circle with a −.

10. Draw a similar path from the positive leg into the other circle. Mark this circle with a +.

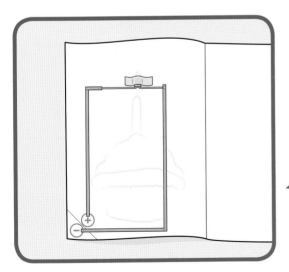

11. Lay down copper tape along the paths you drew in steps 9 and 10. This will form the circuit connecting the LED to the battery.

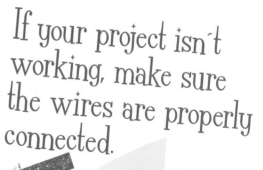

If your project isn't working, make sure the wires are properly connected.

Use It and Test It!

Now it's time to light up your card. Place the battery on the + circle, with the battery's + side down. Fold the corner over it. The candle on your birthday card should start glowing! Once the battery is in place, use the binder clip to secure it and keep the light on.

Change It!

You can create a variety of cards using these techniques. Try the ideas below. What differences do you think each change will cause? Test them out. What differences do you notice? Why do you think those differences occur?

- Add a second LED light, but use only one battery.
- Add additional lights and batteries.
- Try different colors of LED lights.
- Use different types of paper, such as construction paper or cardstock.

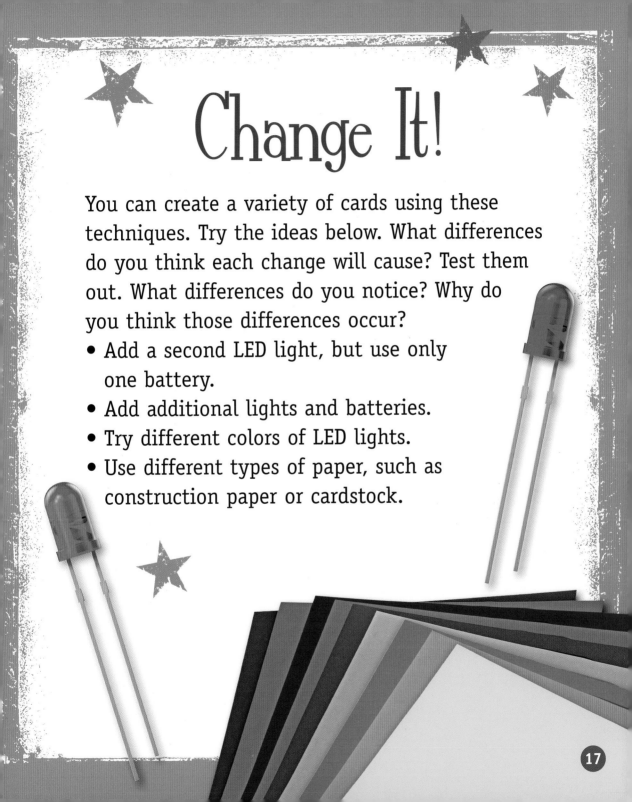

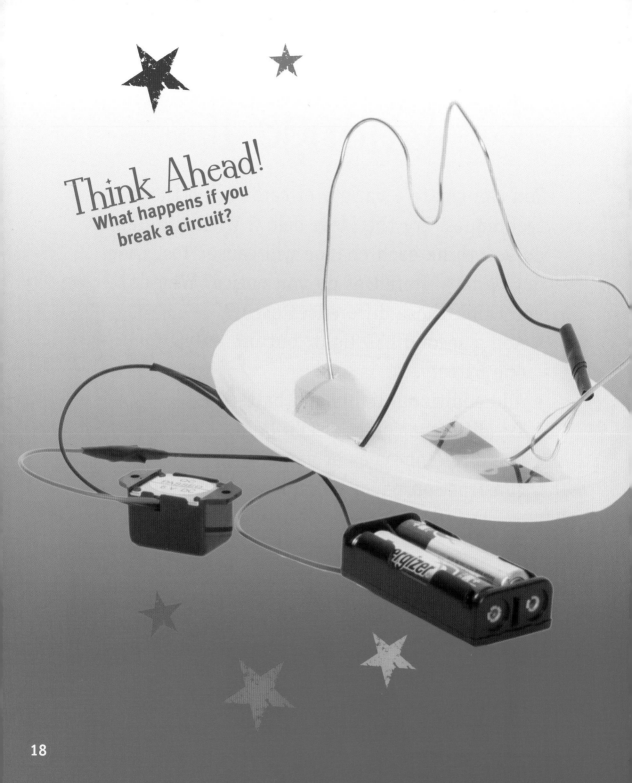

Think Ahead!

What happens if you break a circuit?

CHAPTER 2

Steady Hand Game

How steady is your hand? The game you'll create in this project will help you find out and maybe even improve your skills. Can you move a wire loop around all the twists and turns of a larger wire without making the buzzer go off? Compete with your friends to see who is the fastest and steadiest. Gather your supplies, take a seat in your makerspace, and get to work!

Batteries like the ones used in this project were invented in the 1950s.

Insulation around the copper keeps the electricity from escaping.

Copper wire carries (conducts) electricity.

The wires that run throughout your home and power your appliances have both conducting and insulating materials.

Conductors and Insulators

Some materials, such as metals, are **conductors**. This means electricity can travel through them. Other materials, such as plastic and rubber, are **insulators**. They block electricity from flowing. By combining conductors and insulators in different ways, you can control the path electricity takes as it moves through a circuit.

Incomplete Circuits

As we learned in chapter 1, circuits must form a complete, closed path. If a path is broken, or incomplete, the circuit will not work. In this project, you will build an incomplete circuit. Touching the two wires to each other will close the circuit. This will make the buzzer sound.

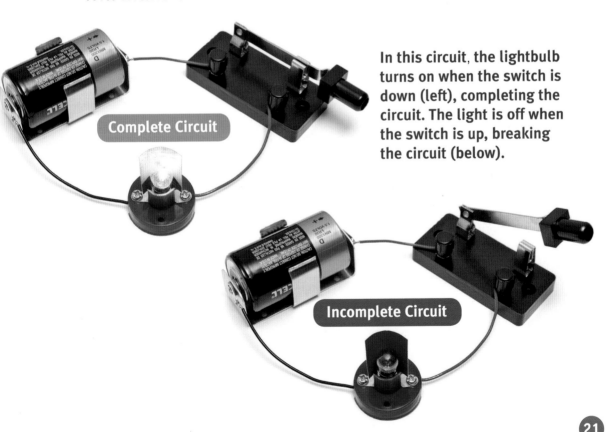

Complete Circuit

Incomplete Circuit

In this circuit, the lightbulb turns on when the switch is down (left), completing the circuit. The light is off when the switch is up, breaking the circuit (below).

Build a Hand Game

What You Need

- ☐ Scissors
- ☐ Small plastic container with lid
- ☐ 12 inches (30.5 centimeters) of 16-gauge bare copper wire
- ☐ Wire stripper
- ☐ AAA battery holder with wires, on/off switch, and slots for two batteries
- ☐ DC 3-24-volt electronic buzzer with wires
- ☐ 14 inches (35.6 cm) of 22-gauge insulated copper wire
- ☐ Electrical tape
- ☐ 2 AAA batteries

Make sure your plastic container is big enough to hold the batteries and buzzer.

Project Instructions

1. With the scissors, poke two small holes at least 2 inches (5 cm) apart in the container's lid.

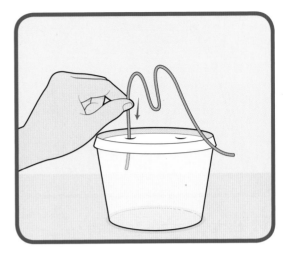

2. Bend the bare copper wire into a curvy shape, such as an M. Push one end down through a hole in the lid.

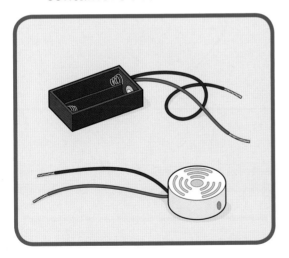

3. Using the wire stripper, strip 0.5 inch (1.3 cm) of insulation from the ends of the battery holder's and buzzer's wires.

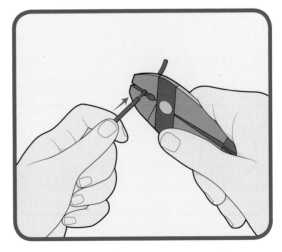

4. Do the same to one end of the insulated wire.

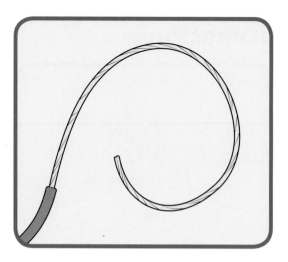

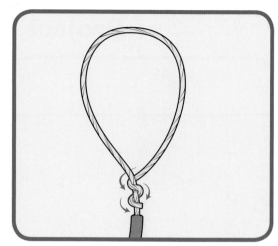

5. Strip 4 inches (10 cm) from the other end of the insulated wire.

6. Bend the stripped end into a loop and twist it onto itself. Wrap electrical tape around the connection.

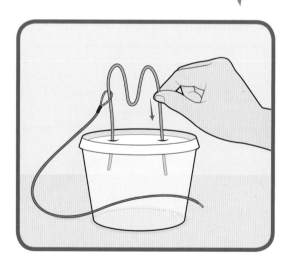

7. Thread the loop onto the bare wire shape. Push the loose end of the bare wire down through the second hole in the container lid.

8. Poke a third hole in the lid. Push the non-looped end of the insulated wire down through it.

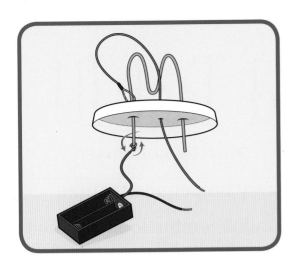

9. Turn the lid over. Twist the stripped end of the battery holder's red wire around one bare wire tip.

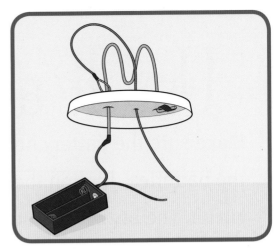

10. Secure with electrical tape. Tape the remaining bare wire end to the lid.

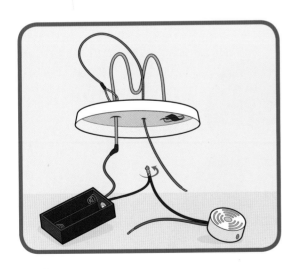

11. Twist together the stripped ends of the battery holder's and buzzer's black wires. Secure with electrical tape.

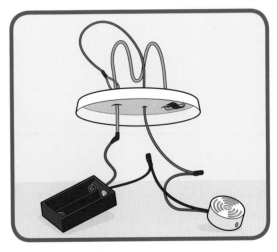

12. Twist together the stripped ends of the buzzer's red wire and the insulated wire. Secure with electrical tape.

Use It and Test It!

Make sure the battery holder is switched off. Insert the batteries. Turn on the battery holder and test the circuit. The buzzer should sound when the loop touches the bare wire. If it doesn't, check that the correct wires are connected to one another and that the batteries are positioned correctly. Once the circuit works, try to move the loop from one end of the bare wire to the other without setting off the buzzer.

Change It!

Experiment with your game to make it different or more challenging. Try making some of the adjustments listed below. What changes do you think each adjustment will cause? Test them out. What differences do you notice? Why do you think those changes occur?

- Change the shape of the bare copper wire.
- Make the loop on the insulated wire smaller or larger.
- Use an LED light instead of the buzzer, or use both at the same time.

Thomas Edison's Bright Ideas

With more than 1,000 **patents** to his name, Thomas Edison is one of the most famous inventors of all time. Many of his incredible creations involved electricity. Here are a few of his greatest hits.

Electrographic Voting Machine

One of Edison's earliest inventions was an electronic voting machine. He patented the device in 1869. Government officials had always had to say "yes" or "no" aloud when voting on new laws. But with Edison's machine, they could simply flip a switch. Unfortunately, the device was not very reliable.

Phonograph

While experimenting with telephone technology in 1877, Edison discovered a way to record his voice. When he spoke into a microphone, the vibrations of the sound moved a needle. The needle etched the vibrations into tinfoil. Later, another needle could be run across these etchings to play the sound back. This led to the creation of phonographs.

Lightbulb

Most lamps in the 1870s burned natural gas to create light. Edison wanted to use electricity instead. By 1879, he had created an electric lightbulb that could be made cheaply and last a long time. As electricity became more available, lightbulbs became the main way people lit up dark areas.

Motion Picture Camera

After recording sound, Edison wanted to record things that could be seen. He and employees at his laboratory built a working movie camera by the early 1890s. The movies it made were silent and about half a minute long. They were an important step in the development of movies as we know them today.

Think Ahead!
How will you design a circuit
that fits in a flashlight?

CHAPTER 3

Homemade Flashlight

Now let's try something a little more complicated. In this project, you'll apply your maker abilities to create a very useful tool: a flashlight. Your flashlight will even have a switch so you can turn it on and off. To complete it, you will need to use all the skills you've learned so far. Let's put it together.

The first flashlights were invented in the 1890s.

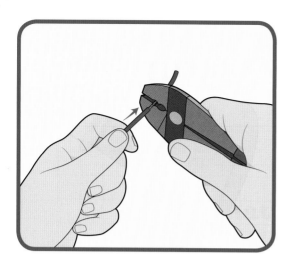

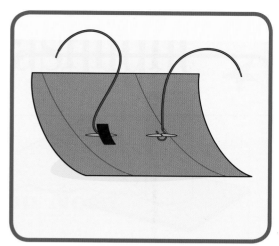

5. Strip 0.5 inch (1.3 cm) of insulation from the ends of each copper wire.

6. Attach the stripped end of a wire to each fastener inside the cardboard roll with electrical tape.

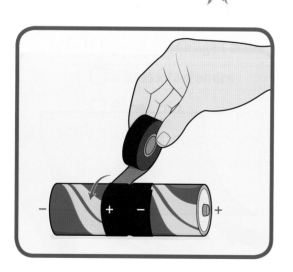

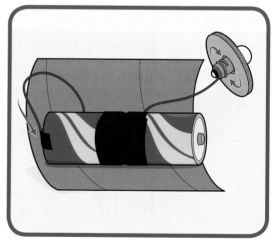

7. Using electrical tape, attach one battery's positive end to the other battery's negative end.

8. Wrap one loose wire end around the metal part of the lightbulb. Tape the remaining wire to the negative end of the batteries with electrical tape.

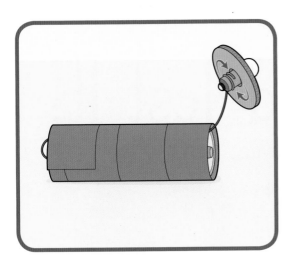

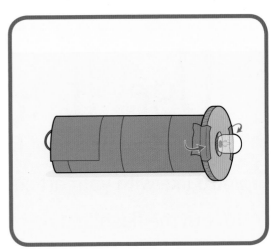

9. Wrap the cardboard tube around the batteries and close with duct tape.

10. Duct tape the cardboard circle to one end of the tube. The metal part of the lightbulb should touch the positive end of the batteries.

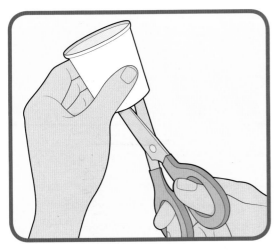

11. Cut a hole in the bottom of the paper cup and poke the lightbulb through. Then duct tape the bottom of the cup to the end of the flashlight.

Use It and Test It!

Decorate your flashlight however you'd like with your art supplies. To turn the flashlight on and off, move the paper clip so it touches both fasteners. This completes the circuit. Is your flashlight shining brightly? If not, make sure everything is connected properly. The lightbulb will turn on only if the batteries are properly aligned with the positive and negative ends in the correct places.

Change It!

You can change your flashlight's brightness, size, or other traits with some experimentation. Try the ideas below. What differences do you think each adjustment will cause? Test them out. What differences do you notice? Why do you think those differences occur?

- Add another battery.
- Use C batteries instead of D.
- Use a larger drinking cup.
- Put aluminum foil in the cup behind the lightbulb.

Famous Inventors and Pioneers

Andre Marie Ampere

(1775–1836) was a French scientist who discovered how electricity and magnetism relate to each other. The ampere, another unit of measuring electricity, is named after him.

Alessandro Volta

(1745–1827) was an Italian inventor who created the first electric battery. The volt, a unit of measuring electricity, is named for him.

Michael Faraday

(1791–1867) was an English physicist and chemist. He was the first person to generate electricity using a magnetic field.

Conrad Hubert

(1855–1928) was a Russian-American inventor who created some of the earliest electric flashlights. He also co-founded the Eveready battery company.

Nikola Tesla

(1856–1943) was a Serbian-American inventor who made many important advances in the study of electricity. His work helped lead to the widespread use of alternating current. This type of electricity is the one used in homes and businesses today.

Elon Musk

(1971–) is an American who leads several forward-thinking technology companies. He is perhaps best known for Tesla Motors, an electric car company, and SpaceX, a company that aims to make space travel available to any paying customer.

Timeline

Benjamin Franklin proves that lightning is electricity.

The first always-on electric light is demonstrated.

1752 **1800** **1835**

Alessandro Volta invents the electric battery.

Thomas Edison opens a central power plant in New York City, the first in the United States.

1879

1882

1950

Almost all parts of the United States have access to electricity.

Thomas Edison invents the practical lightbulb.

True Statistics

Average amount per month a U.S. household spends on electricity: $114.03

Number of batteries sold each year in the United States: About 3 billion

Percentage of energy produced by fossil fuels (oil, gas, and coal) in the United States: 89

Percentage of energy produced by alternative sources (solar, wind, etc.) in the United States: 11

Life span of Edison's 1879 lightbulb: 14.5 hours

Life span of a modern LED lightbulb: 25,000 to 50,000 hours

Life span of the longest burning lightbulb in history: More than 100 years; it has been burning at a fire station in Livermore, California, since 1901

Did you find the truth?

(T) A circuit must form a complete, closed loop.

(F) Conductors are materials that block electricity from moving.

Resources

Books

Nydal Dahl, Øyvind. *Electronics for Kids: Play With Simple Circuits and Experiment With Electricity!* San Francisco: No Starch Press, 2016.

Platt, Charles. *Make: Electronics*. Sebastopol, CA: Maker Media Inc., 2015.

Roland, James. *How Circuits Work*. Minneapolis: Lerner Publications, 2017.

Visit this Scholastic website for more information on electricity:
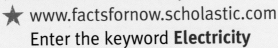 www.factsfornow.scholastic.com
Enter the keyword **Electricity**

Important Words

circuits (SUR-kits) complete paths for electrical currents

components (kuhm-POH-nuhnts) parts of a larger whole, especially a machine, electrical circuit, or system

conductors (kuhn-DUHK-turz) substances that allow electricity to travel through them

insulators (IN-suh-late-urz) substances that stop electricity from moving or escaping

LED (EL-EE-DEE) a low-level, long-lasting, and energy-efficient type of light; LED stands for "light-emitting diode"

makerspace (MAY-kur-spays) any place where people plan, design, tinker, create, change, and fix things for fun or to solve problems

parallel (PAR-uh-lel) staying the same distance from each other and never crossing or meeting

patents (PAT-uhnts) legal documents giving the inventor of an item the sole rights to manufacture or sell it

Index

Page numbers in **bold** indicate illustrations.

About the Author

Kristina A. Holzweiss was selected by *School Library Journal* as the School Librarian of the Year in 2015. She is the founder of SLIME—Students of Long Island Maker Expo—and the president of Long Island LEADS, a nonprofit organization to promote STEAM education and the maker movement. In her free time, Kristina enjoys making memories with her husband, Mike, and their three children, Tyler, Riley, and Lexy.

Scholastic Library Publishing wants to especially thank Kristina A. Holzweiss, Bay Shore Middle School, and all the kids who worked as models in these books for their time and generosity.

PHOTOGRAPHS ©: 4 LEDs and throughout: scanrail/iStockphoto; 4 crayons and throughout: George Filyagin/Shutterstock; 5 top: Marek Mnich/iStockphoto; 5 battery and throughout: Kotkot32/Shutterstock; 5 bottom right: MNI/Shutterstock; 10: Marek Mnich/iStockphoto; 11: scanrail/iStockphoto; 12 markers and throughout: photosync/Shutterstock; 12 graph paper and throughout: billnoll/iStockphoto; 17 bottom right: Eplisterra/iStockphoto; 20: Antonio Gravante/Dreamstime; 21 left: GIPhotoStock/Science Source; 21 right: GIPhotoStock/Science Source; 22 right: Marsel307/Dreamstime; 28-29 background: 4Max/Shutterstock; 28 main: Mondadori Portfolio/Getty Images; 29 top left: SPL/Science Source; 29 top right: -Oxford-/iStockphoto; 29 bottom left: Science & Society Picture Library/Getty Images; 29 bottom right: Bettmann/Getty Images; 32 -33: Designua/Shutterstock; 34 bottom left: Ilya Andriyanov/Shutterstock; 39 left: a_v_d/Shutterstock; 40 left: Sarin Images/The Granger Collection; 40 right: Popperfoto/Getty Images; 41 top: Stock Montage/Getty Images; 41 bottom left: Jacques Boyer/Roger Viollet/Getty Images; 41 bottom right: Dan Tuffs/Getty Images; 42 top left: joecicak/iStockphoto; 42 top right: Billion Photos/Shutterstock; 42 bottom: Sarin Images/The Granger Collection; 43 top: Eric Cohen/Science Source; 43 bottom left: Everett Historical/Shutterstock; 43 bottom right: Sueddeutsche Zeitung Photo/Alamy Images; 44: Science & Society Picture Library/Getty Images.

All instructional illustrations by Brown Bird Design.
All other images by Bianca Alexis Photography.

OCT 3 1 2018